Travel Journal

go where you feel most alive

TRAVEL Bucket List

PLACES I WANT TO VISIT:

THINGS I WANT TO SEE:

TOP 3 DESTINATIONS:

TRIP Itinerary

DESTINATION:	DATE:

MON

TUE

WED

THU

FRI

SAT

SUN

TRAVEL Information

HOTEL INFORMATION

NAME OF HOTEL:

ADDRESS:

PHONE NUMBER:

CONFIRMATION #:

RATE PER NIGHT:

FLIGHT INFORMATION

AIRLINE:

LOCATION:

FLIGHT #:

CHECK IN TIME:

DEPARTURE TIME:

REFERENCE #:

NOTES

TRAVEL Information

CAR RENTAL INFORMATION

COMPANY:

ADDRESS:

PHONE NUMBER:

CONFIRMATION #:

TOTAL COST:

EVENT INFORMATION

EVENT NAME:

LOCATION:

PHONE NUMBER:

START TIME:

OTHER:

NOTES

TRAVEL Information

HOTEL INFORMATION

NAME OF HOTEL:

ADDRESS:

PHONE NUMBER:

CONFIRMATION #:

RATE PER NIGHT:

FLIGHT INFORMATION

AIRLINE:

LOCATION:

FLIGHT #:

CHECK IN TIME:

DEPARTURE TIME:

REFERENCE #:

NOTES

Bon Voyage

TRAVEL Planner

PRE-TRAVEL CHECKLIST

1 MONTH BEFORE

- [ ]
- [ ]
- [ ]
- [ ]
- [ ]

2 WEEKS BEFORE

- [ ]
- [ ]
- [ ]
- [ ]
- [ ]

1 WEEK BEFORE

- [ ]
- [ ]
- [ ]
- [ ]
- [ ]

2 DAYS BEFORE

- [ ]
- [ ]
- [ ]
- [ ]
- [ ]

24 HOURS BEFORE

- [ ]
- [ ]
- [ ]
- [ ]
- [ ]

DAY OF TRAVEL

- [ ]
- [ ]
- [ ]
- [ ]
- [ ]

TRIP TO DO LIST Countdown

travel addict

OUTFIT Planner

DAY:	DESTINATION:	PACKED:	☐

DAY:

ACTIVITY: _____

OUTFIT: _____

SHOES: _____

ACC: _____

EVENING:

_____

_____

_____

_____

DAY:	DESTINATION:	PACKED:	☐

DAY:

ACTIVITY: _____

OUTFIT: _____

SHOES: _____

ACC: _____

EVENING:

_____

_____

_____

_____

DAY:	DESTINATION:	PACKED:	☐

DAY:

ACTIVITY: _____

OUTFIT: _____

SHOES: _____

ACC: _____

EVENING:

_____

_____

_____

_____

exiting
ADVENTURE

PACKING Check List

DOCUMENTS

- [ ] PASSPORT
- [ ] DRIVER'S LICENSE
- [ ] VISA
- [ ] PLANE TICKETS
- [ ] LOCAL CURRENCY
- [ ] INSURANCE CARD
- [ ] HEALTH CARD
- [ ] OTHER ID
- [ ] HOTEL INFORMATION
- [ ] _____
- [ ] _____

CLOTHING

- [ ] UNDERWEAR / SOCKS
- [ ] SWIM WEAR
- [ ] T-SHIRTS
- [ ] JEANS/PANTS
- [ ] SHORTS
- [ ] SKIRTS / DRESSES
- [ ] JACKET / COAT
- [ ] SLEEPWEAR
- [ ] SHOES
- [ ] _____
- [ ] _____

PERSONAL ITEMS

- [ ] SHAMPOO
- [ ] RAZORS
- [ ] COSMETICS
- [ ] HAIR BRUSH
- [ ] LIP BALM
- [ ] WATER BOTTLE
- [ ] SOAP
- [ ] TOOTHBRUSH
- [ ] JEWELRY
- [ ] _____
- [ ] _____

ELECTRONICS

- [ ] CELL PHONE
- [ ] CHARGER
- [ ] LAPTOP
- [ ] BATTERIES
- [ ] EARPHONES
- [ ] FLASH DRIVE
- [ ] MEMORY CARD
- [ ] _____
- [ ] _____
- [ ] _____

HEALTH & SAFETY

- [ ] HAND SANITIZER
- [ ] SUNSCREEN
- [ ] VITAMIN SUPPLEMENTS
- [ ] BANDAIDS
- [ ] ADVIL/TYLENOL
- [ ] CONTACTS / GLASSES
- [ ] COLD/FLU MEDS
- [ ] _____
- [ ] _____
- [ ] _____

OTHER ESSENTIALS

- [ ] _____
- [ ] _____
- [ ] _____
- [ ] _____
- [ ] _____
- [ ] _____
- [ ] _____
- [ ] _____
- [ ] _____
- [ ] _____

PACKING Check List

OUTWARD Journey Schedule

DATE:

☀ ⛅ 🌦 ☁ ⛈

6

7

8

9

10

11

12

1

2

3

4

5

6

7

8

9

10

11

12

DAY:

NOTES

REMINDERS

DAILY Travel Planner

DATE:	ATTRACTION:

THINGS TO SEE

DATE:	ATTRACTION:

THINGS TO SEE

DAILY Travel Planner

DATE:	ATTRACTION:

THINGS TO SEE

DATE:	ATTRACTION:

THINGS TO SEE

Travel Expense Tracker

DESTINATION: _____   BUDGET GOAL: _____

DATE:	DESCRIPTION:	CURRENCY:	AMOUNT:

TOTAL EXPENSES:

Enjoy every moment

Daily TRAVEL JOURNAL

MON

TUE

WED

THU

Daily TRAVEL JOURNAL

FRI

SAT

SUN

RETURN Journey Schedule

DATE:

DAY:

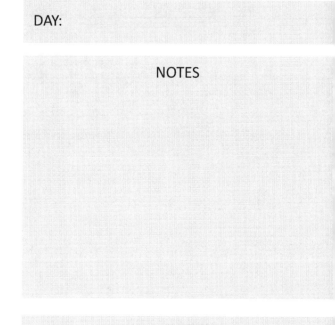

NOTES

6	
7	
8	
9	
10	
11	
12	
1	
2	
3	
4	
5	
6	
7	
8	
9	
10	
11	
12	

REMINDERS

TRAVEL Bucket List

PLACES I WANT TO VISIT:

_____
_____
_____
_____
_____
_____
_____
_____
_____
_____
_____
_____
_____

THINGS I WANT TO SEE:

_____
_____
_____
_____
_____
_____
_____
_____
_____
_____
_____
_____
_____
_____
_____
_____

TOP 3 DESTINATIONS:

_____
_____

TRIP Itinerary

MON

TUE

WED

THU

FRI

SAT

SUN

travel is always a good IDEA

TRAVEL Information

HOTEL INFORMATION

NAME OF HOTEL:

ADDRESS:

PHONE NUMBER:

CONFIRMATION #:

RATE PER NIGHT:

FLIGHT INFORMATION

AIRLINE:

LOCATION:

FLIGHT #:

CHECK IN TIME:

DEPARTURE TIME:

REFERENCE #:

NOTES

TRAVEL Information

COMPANY:

ADDRESS:

PHONE NUMBER:

CONFIRMATION #:

TOTAL COST:

EVENT NAME:

LOCATION:

PHONE NUMBER:

START TIME:

OTHER:

NOTES

TRAVEL Information

HOTEL INFORMATION

NAME OF HOTEL:

ADDRESS:

PHONE NUMBER:

CONFIRMATION #:

RATE PER NIGHT:

FLIGHT INFORMATION

AIRLINE:

LOCATION:

FLIGHT #:

CHECK IN TIME:

DEPARTURE TIME:

REFERENCE #:

NOTES

Bon Voyage

TRAVEL Planner

PRE-TRAVEL CHECKLIST

1 MONTH BEFORE	2 WEEKS BEFORE
☐ _____	☐ _____
☐ _____	☐ _____
☐ _____	☐ _____
☐ _____	☐ _____
☐ _____	☐ _____

1 WEEK BEFORE	2 DAYS BEFORE
☐ _____	☐ _____
☐ _____	☐ _____
☐ _____	☐ _____
☐ _____	☐ _____
☐ _____	☐ _____

24 HOURS BEFORE	DAY OF TRAVEL
☐ _____	☐ _____
☐ _____	☐ _____
☐ _____	☐ _____
☐ _____	☐ _____
☐ _____	☐ _____

TRIP TO DO LIST Countdown

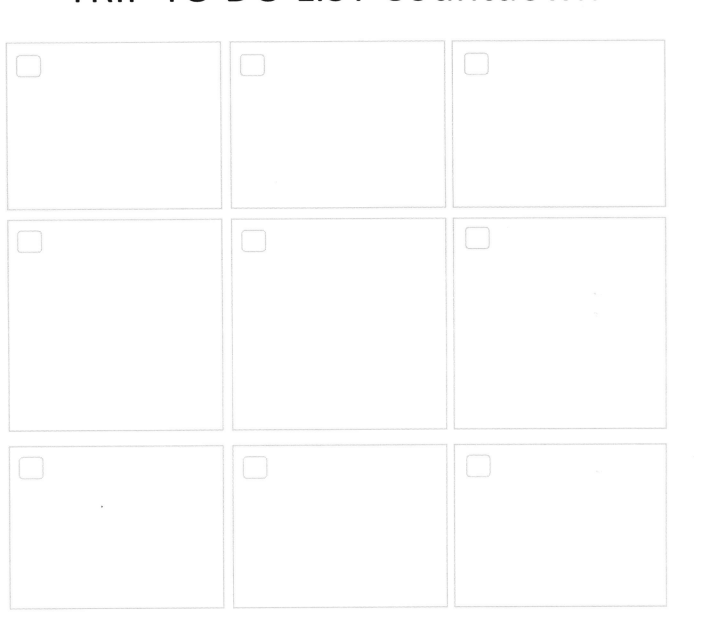

OUTFIT Planner

DAY:	DESTINATION:	PACKED:

DAY:

ACTIVITY: _____

OUTFIT: _____

SHOES: _____

ACC: _____

EVENING:

_____

_____

_____

_____

DAY:	DESTINATION:	PACKED:

DAY:

ACTIVITY: _____

OUTFIT: _____

SHOES: _____

ACC: _____

EVENING:

_____

_____

_____

_____

DAY:	DESTINATION:	PACKED:

DAY:

ACTIVITY: _____

OUTFIT: _____

SHOES: _____

ACC: _____

EVENING:

_____

_____

_____

_____

exiting

ADVENTURE

PACKING Check List

DOCUMENTS

- ☐ PASSPORT
- ☐ DRIVER'S LICENSE
- ☐ VISA
- ☐ PLANE TICKETS
- ☐ LOCAL CURRENCY
- ☐ INSURANCE CARD
- ☐ HEALTH CARD
- ☐ OTHER ID
- ☐ HOTEL INFORMATION
- ☐ _____
- ☐ _____

CLOTHING

- ☐ UNDERWEAR / SOCKS
- ☐ SWIM WEAR
- ☐ T-SHIRTS
- ☐ JEANS/PANTS
- ☐ SHORTS
- ☐ SKIRTS / DRESSES
- ☐ JACKET / COAT
- ☐ SLEEPWEAR
- ☐ SHOES
- ☐ _____
- ☐ _____

PERSONAL ITEMS

- ☐ SHAMPOO
- ☐ RAZORS
- ☐ COSMETICS
- ☐ HAIR BRUSH
- ☐ LIP BALM
- ☐ WATER BOTTLE
- ☐ SOAP
- ☐ TOOTHBRUSH
- ☐ JEWELRY
- ☐ _____
- ☐ _____

ELECTRONICS

- ☐ CELL PHONE
- ☐ CHARGER
- ☐ LAPTOP
- ☐ BATTERIES
- ☐ EARPHONES
- ☐ FLASH DRIVE
- ☐ MEMORY CARD
- ☐ _____
- ☐ _____
- ☐ _____

HEALTH & SAFETY

- ☐ HAND SANITIZER
- ☐ SUNSCREEN
- ☐ VITAMIN SUPPLEMENTS
- ☐ BANDAIDS
- ☐ ADVIL/TYLENOL
- ☐ CONTACTS / GLASSES
- ☐ COLD/FLU MEDS
- ☐ _____
- ☐ _____
- ☐ _____

OTHER ESSENTIALS

- ☐ _____
- ☐ _____
- ☐ _____
- ☐ _____
- ☐ _____
- ☐ _____
- ☐ _____
- ☐ _____
- ☐ _____
- ☐ _____

PACKING Check List

OUTWARD Journey Schedule

DATE:

DAY:

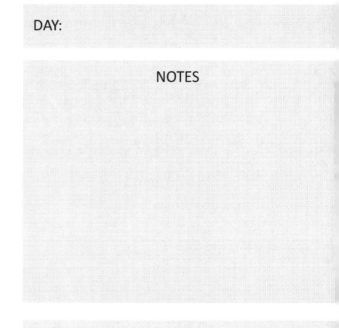

6

7

8

9

10

11

12

1

2

3

4

5

6

7

8

9

10

11

12

NOTES

REMINDERS

DAILY Travel Planner

DATE:	ATTRACTION:

THINGS TO SEE

DATE:	ATTRACTION:

THINGS TO SEE

DAILY Travel Planner

DATE:	ATTRACTION:

THINGS TO SEE

DATE:	ATTRACTION:

THINGS TO SEE

Travel Expense Tracker

DESTINATION: _____   BUDGET GOAL: _____

DATE:	DESCRIPTION:	CURRENCY:	AMOUNT:
	TOTAL EXPENSES:		

Enjoy every moment

Daily TRAVEL JOURNAL

MON

TUE

WED

THU

Daily TRAVEL JOURNAL

FRI

SAT

SUN

RETURN Journey Schedule

DATE:	DAY:

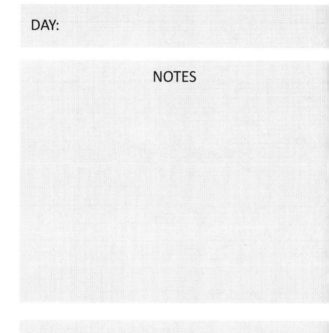

NOTES

6

7

8

9

10

11

12

1

2

3

4

5

6

7

8

9

10

11

12

REMINDERS

TRAVEL Bucket List

PLACES I WANT TO VISIT:

THINGS I WANT TO SEE:

TOP 3 DESTINATIONS:

TRIP Itinerary

DESTINATION:	DATE:

MON

TUE

WED

THU

FRI

SAT

SUN

TRAVEL Information

HOTEL INFORMATION

NAME OF HOTEL:

ADDRESS:

PHONE NUMBER:

CONFIRMATION #:

RATE PER NIGHT:

FLIGHT INFORMATION

AIRLINE:

LOCATION:

FLIGHT #:

CHECK IN TIME:

DEPARTURE TIME:

REFERENCE #:

NOTES

TRAVEL Information

CAR RENTAL INFORMATION

COMPANY:

ADDRESS:

PHONE NUMBER:

CONFIRMATION #:

TOTAL COST:

EVENT INFORMATION

EVENT NAME:

LOCATION:

PHONE NUMBER:

START TIME:

OTHER:

NOTES

TRAVEL Information

HOTEL INFORMATION

NAME OF HOTEL:

ADDRESS:

PHONE NUMBER:

CONFIRMATION #:

RATE PER NIGHT:

FLIGHT INFORMATION

AIRLINE:

LOCATION:

FLIGHT #:

CHECK IN TIME:

DEPARTURE TIME:

REFERENCE #:

NOTES

Bon Voyage

TRAVEL Planner

PRE-TRAVEL CHECKLIST

1 MONTH BEFORE

- [ ]
- [ ]
- [ ]
- [ ]
- [ ]

2 WEEKS BEFORE

- [ ]
- [ ]
- [ ]
- [ ]
- [ ]

1 WEEK BEFORE

- [ ]
- [ ]
- [ ]
- [ ]
- [ ]

2 DAYS BEFORE

- [ ]
- [ ]
- [ ]
- [ ]
- [ ]

24 HOURS BEFORE

- [ ]
- [ ]
- [ ]
- [ ]
- [ ]

DAY OF TRAVEL

- [ ]
- [ ]
- [ ]
- [ ]
- [ ]

TRIP TO DO LIST Countdown

OUTFIT Planner

DAY:	DESTINATION:	PACKED: ☐

DAY:

ACTIVITY: _____

OUTFIT: _____

SHOES: _____

ACC: _____

EVENING:

_____

_____

_____

_____

DAY:	DESTINATION:	PACKED: ☐

DAY:

ACTIVITY: _____

OUTFIT: _____

SHOES: _____

ACC: _____

EVENING:

_____

_____

_____

_____

DAY:	DESTINATION:	PACKED: ☐

DAY:

ACTIVITY: _____

OUTFIT: _____

SHOES: _____

ACC: _____

EVENING:

_____

_____

_____

_____

exiting
ADVENTURE

PACKING Check List

DOCUMENTS

- [ ] PASSPORT
- [ ] DRIVER'S LICENSE
- [ ] VISA
- [ ] PLANE TICKETS
- [ ] LOCAL CURRENCY
- [ ] INSURANCE CARD
- [ ] HEALTH CARD
- [ ] OTHER ID
- [ ] HOTEL INFORMATION
- [ ] _____
- [ ] _____

CLOTHING

- [ ] UNDERWEAR / SOCKS
- [ ] SWIM WEAR
- [ ] T-SHIRTS
- [ ] JEANS/PANTS
- [ ] SHORTS
- [ ] SKIRTS / DRESSES
- [ ] JACKET / COAT
- [ ] SLEEPWEAR
- [ ] SHOES
- [ ] _____
- [ ] _____

PERSONAL ITEMS

- [ ] SHAMPOO
- [ ] RAZORS
- [ ] COSMETICS
- [ ] HAIR BRUSH
- [ ] LIP BALM
- [ ] WATER BOTTLE
- [ ] SOAP
- [ ] TOOTHBRUSH
- [ ] JEWELRY
- [ ] _____
- [ ] _____

ELECTRONICS

- [ ] CELL PHONE
- [ ] CHARGER
- [ ] LAPTOP
- [ ] BATTERIES
- [ ] EARPHONES
- [ ] FLASH DRIVE
- [ ] MEMORY CARD
- [ ] _____
- [ ] _____
- [ ] _____

HEALTH & SAFETY

- [ ] HAND SANITIZER
- [ ] SUNSCREEN
- [ ] VITAMIN SUPPLEMENTS
- [ ] BANDAIDS
- [ ] ADVIL/TYLENOL
- [ ] CONTACTS / GLASSES
- [ ] COLD/FLU MEDS
- [ ] _____
- [ ] _____
- [ ] _____

OTHER ESSENTIALS

- [ ] _____
- [ ] _____
- [ ] _____
- [ ] _____
- [ ] _____
- [ ] _____
- [ ] _____
- [ ] _____
- [ ] _____

PACKING Check List

OUTWARD Journey Schedule

DATE:	DAY:

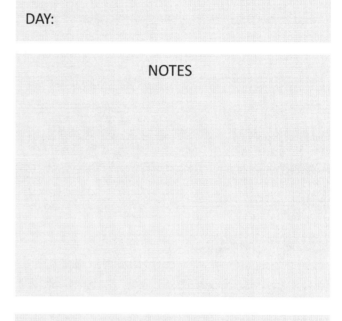

6

7

8

9

10

11

12

1

2

3

4

5

6

7

8

9

10

11

12

NOTES

REMINDERS

DAILY Travel Planner

DATE:	ATTRACTION:

THINGS TO SEE

DATE:	ATTRACTION:

THINGS TO SEE

DAILY Travel Planner

DATE:	ATTRACTION:

THINGS TO SEE

DATE:	ATTRACTION:

THINGS TO SEE

Travel Expense Tracker

DESTINATION: _____   BUDGET GOAL: _____

DATE:	DESCRIPTION:	CURRENCY:	AMOUNT:

TOTAL EXPENSES:

Enjoy every moment

Daily TRAVEL JOURNAL

MON

TUE

WED

THU

Daily TRAVEL JOURNAL

FRI

_____
_____
_____
_____

SAT

_____
_____
_____
_____

SUN

_____
_____
_____
_____

RETURN Journey Schedule

DATE:	DAY:

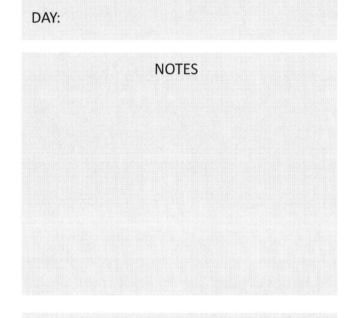

NOTES

6

7

8

9

10

11

12

1

2

3

4

5

6

REMINDERS

7

8

9

10

11

12

TRAVEL Bucket List

PLACES I WANT TO VISIT:

THINGS I WANT TO SEE:

TOP 3 DESTINATIONS:

TRIP Itinerary

DESTINATION:	DATE:

MON

TUE

WED

THU

FRI

SAT

SUN

TRAVEL Information

HOTEL INFORMATION

NAME OF HOTEL:

ADDRESS:

PHONE NUMBER:

CONFIRMATION #:

RATE PER NIGHT:

FLIGHT INFORMATION

AIRLINE:

LOCATION:

FLIGHT #:

CHECK IN TIME:

DEPARTURE TIME:

REFERENCE #:

NOTES

TRAVEL Information

CAR RENTAL INFORMATION

COMPANY:

ADDRESS:

PHONE NUMBER:

CONFIRMATION #:

TOTAL COST:

EVENT INFORMATION

EVENT NAME:

LOCATION:

PHONE NUMBER:

START TIME:

OTHER:

NOTES

TRAVEL Information

HOTEL INFORMATION

NAME OF HOTEL:

ADDRESS:

PHONE NUMBER:

CONFIRMATION #:

RATE PER NIGHT:

FLIGHT INFORMATION

AIRLINE:

LOCATION:

FLIGHT #:

CHECK IN TIME:

DEPARTURE TIME:

REFERENCE #:

NOTES

Bon Voyage

TRAVEL Planner

PRE-TRAVEL CHECKLIST

1 MONTH BEFORE	2 WEEKS BEFORE

1 WEEK BEFORE	2 DAYS BEFORE

24 HOURS BEFORE	DAY OF TRAVEL

TRIP TO DO LIST Countdown

OUTFIT Planner

DAY:	DESTINATION:	PACKED: ☐

DAY:

ACTIVITY: _____

OUTFIT: _____

SHOES: _____

ACC: _____

EVENING:

_____

DAY:	DESTINATION:	PACKED: ☐

DAY:

ACTIVITY: _____

OUTFIT: _____

SHOES: _____

ACC: _____

EVENING:

_____

DAY:	DESTINATION:	PACKED: ☐

DAY:

ACTIVITY: _____

OUTFIT: _____

SHOES: _____

ACC: _____

EVENING:

_____

exiting ADVENTURE

PACKING Check List

DOCUMENTS

- [ ] PASSPORT
- [ ] DRIVER'S LICENSE
- [ ] VISA
- [ ] PLANE TICKETS
- [ ] LOCAL CURRENCY
- [ ] INSURANCE CARD
- [ ] HEALTH CARD
- [ ] OTHER ID
- [ ] HOTEL INFORMATION
- [ ] _____
- [ ] _____

CLOTHING

- [ ] UNDERWEAR / SOCKS
- [ ] SWIM WEAR
- [ ] T-SHIRTS
- [ ] JEANS/PANTS
- [ ] SHORTS
- [ ] SKIRTS / DRESSES
- [ ] JACKET / COAT
- [ ] SLEEPWEAR
- [ ] SHOES
- [ ] _____
- [ ] _____

PERSONAL ITEMS

- [ ] SHAMPOO
- [ ] RAZORS
- [ ] COSMETICS
- [ ] HAIR BRUSH
- [ ] LIP BALM
- [ ] WATER BOTTLE
- [ ] SOAP
- [ ] TOOTHBRUSH
- [ ] JEWELRY
- [ ] _____
- [ ] _____

ELECTRONICS

- [ ] CELL PHONE
- [ ] CHARGER
- [ ] LAPTOP
- [ ] BATTERIES
- [ ] EARPHONES
- [ ] FLASH DRIVE
- [ ] MEMORY CARD
- [ ] _____
- [ ] _____
- [ ] _____

HEALTH & SAFETY

- [ ] HAND SANITIZER
- [ ] SUNSCREEN
- [ ] VITAMIN SUPPLEMENTS
- [ ] BANDAIDS
- [ ] ADVIL/TYLENOL
- [ ] CONTACTS / GLASSES
- [ ] COLD/FLU MEDS
- [ ] _____
- [ ] _____
- [ ] _____

OTHER ESSENTIALS

- [ ] _____
- [ ] _____
- [ ] _____
- [ ] _____
- [ ] _____
- [ ] _____
- [ ] _____
- [ ] _____
- [ ] _____
- [ ] _____

PACKING Check List

OUTWARD Journey Schedule

DATE:

DAY:

☀ ⛅ 🌦 ☁ ⛈

6

7

8

9

10

11

12

1

2

3

4

5

6

7

8

9

10

11

12

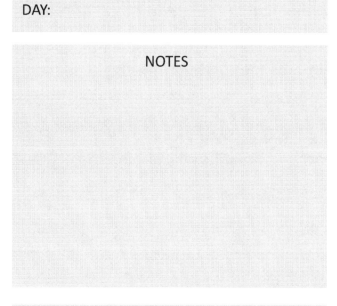

NOTES

REMINDERS

DAILY Travel Planner

DATE:	ATTRACTION:

THINGS TO SEE

DATE:	ATTRACTION:

THINGS TO SEE

DAILY Travel Planner

DATE:	ATTRACTION:

THINGS TO SEE

DATE:	ATTRACTION:

THINGS TO SEE

Travel Expense Tracker

DESTINATION: _____   BUDGET GOAL: _____

DATE:	DESCRIPTION:	CURRENCY:	AMOUNT:

TOTAL EXPENSES:

Enjoy every moment

Daily TRAVEL JOURNAL

MON

TUE

WED

THU

Daily TRAVEL JOURNAL

FRI

_____
_____
_____
_____
_____

SAT

_____
_____
_____
_____
_____

SUN

_____
_____
_____
_____
_____

RETURN Journey Schedule

DATE:

DAY:

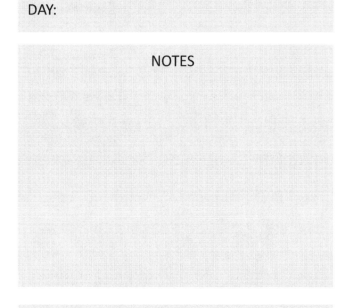

NOTES

6	
7	
8	
9	
10	
11	
12	
1	
2	
3	
4	
5	
6	
7	
8	
9	
10	
11	
12	

REMINDERS

TRAVEL Bucket List

PLACES I WANT TO VISIT:

THINGS I WANT TO SEE:

TOP 3 DESTINATIONS:

TRIP Itinerary

DESTINATION:	DATE:

MON

TUE

WED

THU

FRI

SAT

SUN

TRAVEL Information

HOTEL INFORMATION

NAME OF HOTEL:

ADDRESS:

PHONE NUMBER:

CONFIRMATION #:

RATE PER NIGHT:

FLIGHT INFORMATION

AIRLINE:

LOCATION:

FLIGHT #:

CHECK IN TIME:

DEPARTURE TIME:

REFERENCE #:

NOTES

TRAVEL Information

CAR RENTAL INFORMATION

COMPANY:

ADDRESS:

PHONE NUMBER:

CONFIRMATION #:

TOTAL COST:

EVENT INFORMATION

EVENT NAME:

LOCATION:

PHONE NUMBER:

START TIME:

OTHER:

NOTES

TRAVEL Information

HOTEL INFORMATION

NAME OF HOTEL:

ADDRESS:

PHONE NUMBER:

CONFIRMATION #:

RATE PER NIGHT:

FLIGHT INFORMATION

AIRLINE:

LOCATION:

FLIGHT #:

CHECK IN TIME:

DEPARTURE TIME:

REFERENCE #:

NOTES

Bon Voyage

TRAVEL Planner

PRE-TRAVEL CHECKLIST

1 MONTH BEFORE

- [ ]
- [ ]
- [ ]
- [ ]
- [ ]

2 WEEKS BEFORE

- [ ]
- [ ]
- [ ]
- [ ]
- [ ]

1 WEEK BEFORE

- [ ]
- [ ]
- [ ]
- [ ]
- [ ]

2 DAYS BEFORE

- [ ]
- [ ]
- [ ]
- [ ]
- [ ]

24 HOURS BEFORE

- [ ]
- [ ]
- [ ]
- [ ]
- [ ]

DAY OF TRAVEL

- [ ]
- [ ]
- [ ]
- [ ]
- [ ]

TRIP TO DO LIST Countdown

☐

☐

☐

☐

☐

☐

☐

☐

☐

travel addict

OUTFIT Planner

DAY:	DESTINATION:	PACKED: ☐

DAY:

ACTIVITY: ....

OUTFIT: ....

SHOES: ....

ACC: ....

EVENING:

....

....

....

....

DAY:	DESTINATION:	PACKED: ☐

DAY:

ACTIVITY: ....

OUTFIT: ....

SHOES: ....

ACC: ....

EVENING:

....

....

....

....

DAY:	DESTINATION:	PACKED: ☐

DAY:

ACTIVITY: ....

OUTFIT: ....

SHOES: ....

ACC: ....

EVENING:

....

....

....

....

exiting

ADVENTURE

PACKING Check List

DOCUMENTS

- [ ] PASSPORT
- [ ] DRIVER'S LICENSE
- [ ] VISA
- [ ] PLANE TICKETS
- [ ] LOCAL CURRENCY
- [ ] INSURANCE CARD
- [ ] HEALTH CARD
- [ ] OTHER ID
- [ ] HOTEL INFORMATION
- [ ] _____
- [ ] _____

CLOTHING

- [ ] UNDERWEAR / SOCKS
- [ ] SWIM WEAR
- [ ] T-SHIRTS
- [ ] JEANS/PANTS
- [ ] SHORTS
- [ ] SKIRTS / DRESSES
- [ ] JACKET / COAT
- [ ] SLEEPWEAR
- [ ] SHOES
- [ ] _____
- [ ] _____

PERSONAL ITEMS

- [ ] SHAMPOO
- [ ] RAZORS
- [ ] COSMETICS
- [ ] HAIR BRUSH
- [ ] LIP BALM
- [ ] WATER BOTTLE
- [ ] SOAP
- [ ] TOOTHBRUSH
- [ ] JEWELRY
- [ ] _____
- [ ] _____

ELECTRONICS

- [ ] CELL PHONE
- [ ] CHARGER
- [ ] LAPTOP
- [ ] BATTERIES
- [ ] EARPHONES
- [ ] FLASH DRIVE
- [ ] MEMORY CARD
- [ ] _____
- [ ] _____
- [ ] _____

HEALTH & SAFETY

- [ ] HAND SANITIZER
- [ ] SUNSCREEN
- [ ] VITAMIN SUPPLEMENTS
- [ ] BANDAIDS
- [ ] ADVIL/TYLENOL
- [ ] CONTACTS / GLASSES
- [ ] COLD/FLU MEDS
- [ ] _____
- [ ] _____
- [ ] _____

OTHER ESSENTIALS

- [ ] _____
- [ ] _____
- [ ] _____
- [ ] _____
- [ ] _____
- [ ] _____
- [ ] _____
- [ ] _____
- [ ] _____
- [ ] _____

PACKING Check List

OUTWARD Journey Schedule

DATE:

DAY:

☀ ⛅ 🌦 ☁ ⛈

6

7

8

9

10

11

12

1

2

3

4

5

6

7

8

9

10

11

12

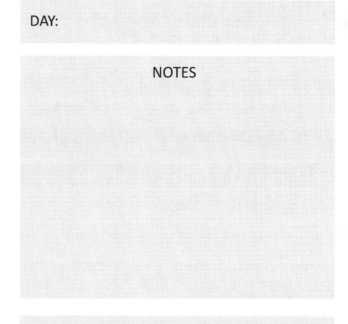

NOTES

REMINDERS

DAILY Travel Planner

DATE:	ATTRACTION:

THINGS TO SEE
☐
☐
☐
☐
☐
☐
☐
☐
☐

DATE:	ATTRACTION:

THINGS TO SEE
☐
☐
☐
☐
☐
☐
☐
☐
☐

DAILY Travel Planner

DATE:	ATTRACTION:

THINGS TO SEE

DATE:	ATTRACTION:

THINGS TO SEE

Travel Expense Tracker

DESTINATION: _____   BUDGET GOAL: _____

DATE:	DESCRIPTION:	CURRENCY:	AMOUNT:

TOTAL EXPENSES:

Enjoy every moment

Daily TRAVEL JOURNAL

MON

TUE

WED

THU

Daily TRAVEL JOURNAL

FRI

SAT

SUN

RETURN Journey Schedule

DATE:	DAY:

	NOTES
6	
7	
8	
9	
10	
11	
12	REMINDERS
1	
2	
3	
4	
5	
6	
7	
8	
9	
10	
11	
12	

Made in United States
Orlando, FL
05 December 2023

40260527R00067